Culling

Also by George Held

Neighbors: The Yard Critters Too
illustrated by Joung Un Kim
New York, NY: Filsinger and Company, 2013

*Neighbors: The Yard Critter*s, Book 1
illustrated by Joung Un Kim
New York, NY: Filsinger and Company, 2011

After Shakespeare: Selected Sonnets
W. Somerville, MA: Červená Barva Press, 2011

Phased
Hoboken, NJ: Poets Wear Prada, 2008

The News Today
W. Somerville, MA: Červená Barva Press, 2008

The Art of Writing and Others
Georgetown, KY: Finishing Line Press, 2007

W Is for War
W. Somerville, MA: Červená Barva Press, 2006

Martial Artist, translator
Claremont, CA: Toad Press, 2005

Grounded
Georgetown, KY: Finishing Line Press, 2005

Untitled e-book
Nashville, TN: *The HyperTexts*, 2004

American Poetry
Farrell, PA: New Formalist Press, 2003

Touched by Eros, editor
Islip, NY: The Live Poets Society, 2002

Beyond Renewal
Mena, AR: Cedar Hill Publications, 2001

Absolut Death and Others
with paintings by Roz Dimon
New York, NY: Dimon Studios, 2000

Open and Shut: Cinquains
Talent, OR: Talent House Press, 1999

Salamander Love and Others
Talent, OR: Talent House Press, 1998

Winged
Northport, NY: Birnham Wood Graphics, 1995

Culling

New & Selected Nature Poems

by
George Held

POETS WEAR PRADA • Hoboken, New Jersey

Culling: New & Selected Nature Poems

Poets Wear Prada
533 Bloomfield Street, Second Floor
Hoboken, New Jersey 07030
http://pwpbooks.blogspot.com

First North American Publication 2014
First Mass Market Paperback Edition 2014

Grateful acknowledgment is made to the following publications where some of these poems have appeared:

The Aurorean; The Blackbird Review; Blue Unicorn; Free Verse; Mid-America Poetry Review; Möbius, The Poetry Magazine; Muddy River Review; The New Verse News; Open Cut; Tiger's Eye; Waterways; Wilderness House Literary Review; Reeds and Rushes (2010); *Paumanok: Poems and Photographs of Long Island* (2009); *Salt Marshes: A Natural and Unnatural History* (2009); *Sag Harbor Is a Literary Celebration* (2006); *Winged* (1995); *Grounded* (2005); *Phased* (2008); *and After Shakespeare: Selected Sonnets* (2011).

ISBN-13: 978-0615910079; ISBN-10: 0615910076
Library of Congress Control Number: 2014903078

Printed in the U.S.A.

Front Cover Image: David Freed
Author Photo: Cheryl Filsinger

For Kathryn and Maryann

And for Roxanne

In memory of Mario D'Avanzo

Table of Contents

Preface

In his profound Cape Cod meditation on the loss of pristine nature, Henry Beston refers to "natural quiet," that state in which one hears only the sounds of the natural world, without the interference of any man-made sound. Today, with world population soaring, natural quiet, as well as pure darkness, is growing rarer, and global warming threatens to banish or drown many species, while "development" extirpates hundreds of them yearly.

Whereas human beings interacted with nature in North America during the reign of the American Indian and in the first two centuries after European settlement, the Industrial Revolution, the extension of civilization to the West, and now the growing urbanization of the nation and the exploitation of natural resources have limited for us the possibility of encountering the natural world directly. "In Wildness is the preservation of the World," wrote Thoreau in the 1850s. Today, we read him and other nature writers, like Henry Beston (1888 – 1968) and Aldo Leopold (1887 – 1948), not with a sense of promise but with nostalgia. They warned us, years ago, that Nature was losing ground to human beings driven by progress and development.

As a poet who often writes about nature, I feel deep love for the woods, animals, and birds I encountered as a boy and still occasionally see or hear today on walks, but more often I write with a sense of loss — loss of habitat, species, quiet, dark — and ultimately with concern for the Earth's well-being. Thus I have culled for this book my nature poems, beginning with those that express affection for the damselfly and the osprey, among other winged creatures, and ending with those on losses, like the melting of European glaciers, the "Glacial Warning" that our ecosystem is undergoing unprecedentedly rapid warming. I hope that readers of these poems will act on a sense of our shared need to conserve what's left of the imperiled natural world.

GH

New York, 5 October 2013

Culling

Winter

The Snow

The snow goes
Right to left
North to south
Past my window

The snow falls
Top to bottom
Heaven to Earth
On my sills

The snow, omen
Of winter death,
Takes my breath
Away every time.

The Hudson

Now he can see it through his bay window,
beyond the January ginkgoes and elms,
the glint of gray-green Hudson at the end
of West 11th Street. That's Jersey
across the river, where on frigid days
in the '40s folks drove cars over the ice,
ice too thick for the dull-gray icebreakers
to chop open a channel to Albany.
Back then he'd lie in the back seat, drowsy
from visiting his Uncle Jacob's flat
in the Village, and gaze up at the George
Washington Bridge, sparkling with lights, no
lower deck thickening its majesty yet,
comforted by the sight, then fall asleep
before the car reached the Henry Hudson
Bridge, on the way back home to Edgemont.

Some summer evenings the family drove
to the Yonkers waterfront near the once
flourishing (now gone) Otis Elevator
factory to watch the sun disappear
behind the Palisades. The scene was like
a picture postcard, gulls and cormorants
fishing off the pilings, and much as he
appreciated their landings and takeoffs
against the sunset, his thoughts would settle
on Giselle, who had gone away to camp
and who'd begun to intrude on his dreams
of Joe DiMaggio and a BB gun
modeled on Red Ryder's repeater carbine.

How many times had he crossed the river
on the Tappan Zee, the Mid-Hudson, the Rip

van Winkle bridges, looked both north and south
at the expanse of water; how many
train trips had he taken along the river bank
to Hudson or to Albany, hooked on
the view of the Catskills, comparable
in life to their images in paintings
of the Hudson River School; how vivid
the scene of mountains and river valley
from Olana, Church's hillside palace
(from which, Church reckoned, before he built,
he would have the best view of the west bank);
driving Route 9, how the signposts for Dutch
or Indian names — Poughkeepsie, Brinckerhoff,
Taghkanic, Kinderhook — had delighted him
along the way. He'd even seen the head-
waters above Glens Falls. For years raw sewage
and GE's PCBs had so poisoned
the waters that by the time they'd reached
the Upper Bay their stink and putrescence
embodied the word "polluted," around
the piers the river barren, good as dead.

But today there is a River Keeper
and regulation of all that gets dumped
into the Hudson, and even the sturgeon
are making a comeback. And he's happy,
because he's wanted the river to come
back, to be able to discharge the clean
waters of the Adirondacks, to be
a vivid testament to the power
of nature running through gorges and past
villages and estates with their moorings,
and under the hulls of sailboats and scows,
and along West Side Highway to the ocean,
and because his imagination has long

sought renewal there in that mighty flow,
the sun now nearly set on the Hudson
as he watches it through his bay window.

Crow(s)

I
I think that I shall never know
A bird as raucous as a crow.

In crows begins responsibility.

Little Crow, who made thee?

II
That dust of snow
From a hemlock tree
A lonely crow
Shook down on me

Has given my skull
A cold white halo:
A winter tableau
In chiaroscuro.

III
Crows don't return in the spring
To raise our spirits;
They hunker down all winter,
Emblems of our limits.

IV
The gregarious crow
Finds home in a rookery,
Does multifarious deeds
Including crookery.

A nefarious symbol
To the superstitious,
As black as the plague he
Calls up images deathly.

    V

I know, said the crow,
folks prefer Allegro,
but I'm Penseroso.

    VI

Crows are also Great Plains Indians
and Crow their Siouan tongue;
hear them crow over the foe
they have routed in battle.

    VII

Caw! Caw! Caw!
Awful the crow's song
and awesome.

    VIII

Crows crowd the suburbs
disturbing sleepers
uprooting robins
cardinals and other songsters.

IX
A roadkill crow
crushed beside a squashed
squirrel: when stealing a bite
keep your head up.

X
Blackness, the culture decrees,
Is the sign of the devil;
Put a bounty on crows in trees,
Each carcass combating evil.

XI
Black bird on white branch —
can the crow see
my breath too?

XII
Crow's feet
nest
next to my
lover's eyes

Crow's nests
perch
atop masts

We quest
for
the essence
of crow ...

   XIII
In the yard
the field
the dump
the snow
struts
the crow.

Birds of a Feather ...

"The common crow, Corvus brachyrhynchos, is the American bird as much as the bald eagle or wild turkey."

        — *Larry Penny*

I. Roosting

Winter's bare branches bear hunched black birds
a thousand or more crows in a roost.

At dawn they fly forth on patrol
scouting, hunting, soaring, circling, scavenging

but of an evening they return to the roost
to gossip and preen, to huddle and rest.

II. Feeding

Where four roads converge in a wood
Crows sit, sentinels scanning
East, south, west, north
Coolly looking for roadkill.

Be it possum, coon, squirrel, or crow
Roadkill means easy pickings
Dining alfresco at asphalt cafés
A picnic where ants serve as canapés.

III. Mobbing

Robins rise from their nest
Mob a crow who made eyes
At their young, chase him
Over the horizon

While a crow-conspirator swoops
To clutch a still-blind baby
From the nest. All that brooding
Leaving the parents to brood.

But let a great horned owl
Prowl near a crow's nest
And these marauders turn
Mobsters themselves, rise

In cacophonous outrage
At this independent predator
And drive her off without fear
Another owl will swoop

To feed upon crow babies.
Birds of a feather who roost
Together find strength in numbers;
A lone wolf might go hungry.

IV. Stealing

Crow has an eye for gewgaws,
Like jays, magpies, and jackdaws.

He's like to steal a bright earring
As eat another bird's fledgling

And deposit it in his bark bank
Like a thrifty saver's paycheck.

He'll build a hoard like a Viking
For whatever he takes a liking

To — a penny, a bone, a pin.
One stole my top but couldn't spin

It, just put it aside for safe-
Keeping. Shouldn't we wonder if

Crow copies us or we ape Crow:
We can say, "Caw," and eat crow.

Scavengers and Predators

When the sun drops behind the fields,
the crows gather downtown
for their nightly convention.

Tens of thousands of them
fly in from every direction,
gather on roofs and in treetops

under the bright lights of city office buildings
and the Auburn Correctional Facility.
The lights help them spot their predators —
hawks and great horned owls.

In February, on a weekend crow shoot,
hunters win cash prizes for killing the most crows,
gather at Spinouts Tavern to count their kills.
Even the winner's 43 dead crows won't put
a dent in the 50,000-crow roost.

Redbird on Black Bough

Cardinal, cloaked in red
Like his Eminence
Whose name you bear;
Principal of all red,

Preening your carmine breast;
Vermilion swatch
On a bare branch;
Coal black mask, blood red crest;

Overwintering, you
Redeem the bleak
Leafless landscape:
Crimson on a black bough.

The Waning Moon

In memory of Dave Church (1947 – 2008)

Moon on the wane,
Ten degrees outside.

Will it wax again
Next month?

Will life renew in spring?
Will the heart stay young?

Those Crocuses

I sowed a year ago
last fall
this spring
break Earth's crust
with promise
of two or three blooms
for every one corm sown.
They'll yearly
multiply
the splendor
in the still-brown grass:
white, yellow,
striped, purple
mini-tulip heads
on two-inch stems
will torque toward
the Marching sun,
that magnet
now drawing
firm leaves
through soil's surface:
then buds emerge,
petals tightly furled,
and then the vernal
revelations
of ochre anthers
within trim cups.

March

Bitter cold, bitter cold, my love,
Winter's sharp tooth pierces glove
And parka, cold shivers our frame,
We make love in vain.

Spring warmth, spring warmth, my dear,
Melts our hearts and brings us cheer;
The bright, clear days grow longer,
Our breasts fill with song.

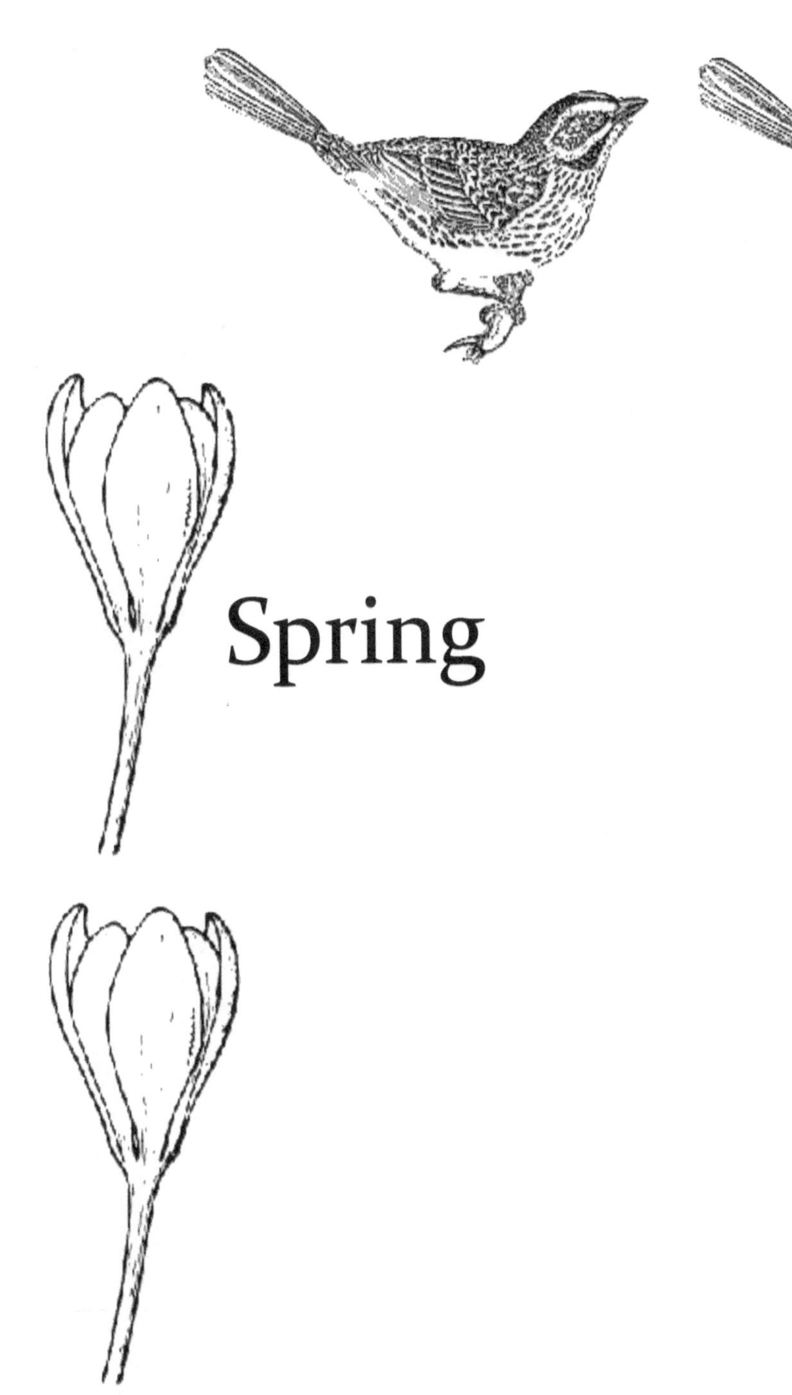

Spring

March 20, 2009

It's snowing the first day of spring —
No big anomaly. Six inches flushed
Me from the garden one April 6th.

Fat flakes drop straight down, trees hushed,
The mercury at 36 degrees.
Small flakes soon slant in a breeze —

The lion growling in a last fling,
Before the lamb gentles the spring.

Names for the March Full Moon

I. The Full Worm Moon

> Days grow milder,
> worm casts rising from thawed earth —
>   robins soon

II. The Full Crow Moon

> Days grow milder,
> Northwoods crows cawing loud —
>   the smell of skunk cabbage

III. The Full Crust Moon

> Days grow milder,
> melting snow, freezing crust at night —
>   the scent of witch hazel

IV. The Full Sap Moon

> Days grow milder,
> maple sap runs, tap dripping —
>   ah, the sweetness

Feeding Chickadees

Black-capped mendicant,
why do you put your life in my hand —
just to snatch an easy snack,
beaking seed from my palm as you straddle
my thumb and forefinger?
Not one extra instant do you linger:
the black cap dips, the sharp beak plucks
a sunflower seed, and you skedaddle
to the nearest branch that's out of reach
to hull your catch,
then "gull" it down
and cast the husk aside.

Chickadee-dee-dee you call,
and the flittering wings of your kin
announce that they've forsaken
sedulous forage for seedy feeding
at this strange pink perch
that wavers slightly
as your feathery ounces weigh upon it,
claws clenching skin,
while I sit on my urge
to snap my fingers
shut like a trap
and have my way with you.

See-saw, see-saw call your kin
from the depths of the wood
as I make my way out,
dark urges pressed down,
buoyed by the impression
of your wild clasp.

Hussey's Woods

I never knew the Husseys
but I knew well Hussey's Woods,
mainly the white pine so tall and wide
nothing but needles grew on the ground below.

That tree stood up for me when
I'd refuse the razor strop
my father's wine-dark rage sought to snap
across my butt, and run from home to the woods.

Panicked and panting I plunged
through thicket, briars tearing
trousers and skin, till out of hearing,
safe beneath the pine tree's boughs deep in the woods.

At the giant's base, my back
against its trunk, heels planted
in soft needle mulch, I sucked scented
breath of pine as my pulse eased, home in the woods.

I'd rise stiff and hug the tree,
resin sticking to my shirt
and cheek, cool bark hard against my heart,
as I felt the worth of all that homely woods.

Now no tree or shrub remains —
only the macadam car lot
and showroom of Curtis Chevrolet,
waxed bodies blazing where native woods once stood.

Now any kid growing up
in my place will lack a tree

to back him up, lack earth to breathe free,
on the needles in the heart of Hussey's Woods.

April

If I couldn't finger the damp soil
And spill seed into furrow and hole

If I couldn't hear the song sparrow's trill
And fill again the birdbath bowl

If I couldn't prune my pear and apple trees
And rake up winter's refuse

And if I couldn't bear the blisters
From rake and hoe, or the splinters

If I couldn't bear the bad back
And sore shoulders and hamstrings

If I couldn't stand the torn skin
From cutting back the wild rose

Why would I ache for April as I do
Whenever winter starts to wane?

Green Again

I'd forgotten the green glory of tree leaves
as they break buds after the equinox.

I'd been in a long winter funk,
sunk by my own rejections and losses

when I happened to look out my window
and see the green cast of a maple,

leaves uncurling along every twig,
like daubs of paint in a Monet.

In my gloom I had missed the first green tips
emerge, but now the tree stood transformed

and transformed the landscape and me
from gray of winter to green again.

Greenwich Village Elm with Yellow Belly

I sit reading in my recliner,
Late morning, when a flash
Of color catches my eye
Out the window.

I know right away what it is —
A yellow-bellied sapsucker
On his way north, stopping
Off to peck insects

Out of the rippled bark,
Just as he did on his way south
Last fall. For ten years, twice the span
Of this woodpecker,

A yellow belly has fed
From this sixty-year-old elm.
It must lie in this bird's
Migration flyway.

Like a child, I watch the red spots
On brow and throat, the white bars
On head and wing,
The black-and-white splotches

Low on the yellow breast
Rounding the trunk or boughs
As this harbinger drills orderly holes
Every spring and fall.

April 23

Reflecting that it's Shakespeare's and Nabokov's birthday
I sit by the window watching a gray squirrel
scratch for food buried in my yard.

Digging up a hickory nut, he scurries over to my rail fence,
scrambles up a post and sits on top,
flattens his tail along his spine.

Grasping the nut with both hands, he rotates it
to find the easiest entry point, then gnaws
the shell to bits and eats the meat.

My view framed by the window, I can see the sky no more
than he so focused on his nut and share
in his surprise the second

a red-tailed hawk grasps his spine and lifts
him above my sightline, bits of nut
left on the fence post.

Marsh Marigold
Caltha palustris

In Riverside Park,
Squat like a toad,

You cheer up dreary April
With shiny yellow petals

Above leaves shaped like
Your buttercup cousin's.

Kingcup, your flower
Reflects its sun

Under my wife's chin.

Turtle Stamp

On the panel of "Reptiles & Amphibians" stamps
The ornate box turtle stands between the blue-spotted
salamander and the reticulate collared lizard,
Its starburst carapace dominant, the orange-spotted
Right front leg extended, the head erect,
With orange ear and staring eye.

Fifty years ago lots of box turtles appeared every spring
To mate. As a boy I loved to watch the creature's stately lurch
On sun-dappled ground just warm enough
To warm its body enough so it could move along
In hopes of meeting a mate, and the odds
Were good, such turtles being common as porcupines.

Three years ago I saw one transecting my back yard,
Heading for the small and diminishing woods behind.
I trailed it till it sensed me and sheltered in its shell.
Now a house sits where the woods were, and no mate
To be found. The only habitat left to this prehistoric
Relic is the size of a postage stamp.

Spring Comes Late
Maryland, NY

Spring comes late to Dog Hill Road —
Nighttime temperatures in the 30s
Even late in May,

And when the sun
Strikes the early morning air,
Mist veils the valley —

So we wait till mid-June
To open the trailer and trade
Asphalt for alfalfa.

Sad Birds

The photos of oil-marinated gulls
And pelicans dying in the Gulf
Make me want to see Tony Hayward
Of BP also floating in the shallows

Completely coated with his product,
A stunned look in his oil-glazed eyes,
His rich thick Oxbridge hair stuck
In place with his own tarry gunk,

His featherless baby-skin slicked black
With oil, a drop falling from his beak
As he looks pitifully for succor
From the volunteer wildlife rescuers,

Who size him up for triage and say,
"This sad bird is too far gone to save."

Osprey

Osprey, you can see by the dawn's
       Early light
A fish 'neath the finish of the bay
       In your flight
As you circle and soar or you stall
       Like a kite,
Ever ready to dive on your prey
       When in sight;
Then you drop like a plummet until
       You alight
On the brine with your talons outstretched
       And they bite
Into scales of that silvery bass, lifting it clear
       Of the bight
Of the bay with your ten-horse wings to retake
       The sun's light,
And you land on your platform to tend to your nestling's
       End of night
Hunger, tearing the bass with your terrible beak
       Into bite-
Sized gobbets for your fledgling to gorge on, its break-
       Fast birthright
As your scion, O Osprey, you long-winged king
       Of the heights.

At Home with the Damselfly

> *"I am from the fields, you know, and while quite at home with the dandelion, make a sorry figure in the drawing room."*
>
> — *Emily Dickinson*

You stalk the dragon
and the damselfly
down by the pondside
deep in the woods
where no one else but a fisherman
might alight.

In the marsh grass
you painstakingly creep
up upon a copulating couple
to catch them in the act —
a pair of bluets, say,
he hanging on to a stem
she beneath
inverted like a fishhook
tip of ovipositor flush
against his abdomen or
he hovering like a hummer
she beneath
painstakingly laying her eggs
on the watersmooth surface.

Among those aerial jewels
you lose yourself
the day long
capturing enameled neon specimens
in your lens, at ease
in your boggy acres

where no human intercourse
makes demands you cannot meet.

Summer

Natural Quiet

Ever hear a garter part the green blades,
A hummer's wings whir, a leaf fall in fall,
The "natural ambient sound conditions"
That abound only beyond man's decibels?
Today utility lines' and traffic's hum
Invades the most pristine park lands. Beston[*]
Warned synthetic light would end night's darkness;
Now be warned about the loss of stillness.

I've known natural quiet only once,
In the core of the Swedish forest, where
Lost alongside a lake one moonless night,
Too rapt for fright, I heard cicadas chirr,
Hooves thump, mink drink, fish splash, although the roar
Of blood deafened me, and dark sealed my sight.

---

[*] Henry Beston (1888 – 1968) comments on the loss of "natural ambient sound conditions" in *The Outermost House* (1925).

Red Fox

A whiff of skunk but not so strong
halts my feet, pricks up my ears

I know you're there in the shrubs
like a trope on the tip of my mind

but you do not show yourself
and stay olfactory

I know you haunt the margins
where vole, mouse, and rabbit run

You den in an indention
under a slope of wooded ground

give birth to kits with catlike whiskers
that will home them to the kill

and, coonlike, you raid the hen
house or upend a garbage pail

If you'd let me glimpse your feline
grace I'd stand transfixed

awed as Adam needing to name you:
Fuchs, renard, zorro, liska, fox

sly, crafty fellow who thrives
on the margin, avoiding those

who would turn you into a hat,
a stole, or a winter coat.

Montauk Chiaroscuro

A rock, hump big as a sea turtle,
rides the tide by Montauk Point,
lower-half blacked by wet, upper whitewashed
with guano.

A great black-backed gull struts
on the rock, head and breast white.
A double-crested cormorant, black as
ebony,

lands beside him. They compose the black
chop of sea, the azure sky with cotton
cumulus on the horizon, the gray North Fork,
the bleached beach.

Along the strand six towheads, teens
in black spandex shorts and white T's,
stroll, spy, not the vista, but a target
for their stones ...

The birds, the boys have flown. The clack
of stone on rock yields its echo
to the low hum of a distant
fishing boat.

In the West Woods

A woodpecker drills deep
In the west woods,
Drilling deep into the wood.

I prefer its sound to sparrow's cheep,
Thinking it good
Some bird's understood

My need for going deep
Where none else would.

A Bird's Song

Music
Of a catbird
A morning serenade —
Who needs the nightingale to stir
A life?

To a Tick

You wait upon a slender stalk of grass
for a carefree hiker to brush you off
upon her ankle, thigh, or calf,
from which you'll crawl up to her ass,
like a lover looking for an ingress,
some private niche that's warm, soft, and moist,
where you'll anesthetize your host,
worming your head in to break your fast.

She won't know you're there till it's too late
to stop the spirochete in your sputum:
your subtle parasitic stratagem
makes you blood-bloated to regenerate,
while her blood will require a regime
of penicillin to combat her Lyme.

The Tiger

The tiger prowls the Indian jungle,
Queen of all the vertebrates,
Four hundred pounds of bundled muscle.

Her stripes with the background mingle,
Helping her hide from the prey she awaits;
The tiger prowls the Indian jungle.

Her horny claws lust to entangle
The flesh of a luscious ungulate,
Four hundred pounds of bundled muscle

Breaking its back as they tumble,
Her incisors sunk in its nape.
The tiger prowls the Indian jungle,

Hunger making her belly rumble,
Driven to feed her darling young denmates;
Four hundred pounds of bundled muscle.

O keep your children home; don't bungle,
Lest you let the man-eater celebrate.
The tiger prowls the interior jungle,
Four hundred pounds of bundled muscle.

Lemurs at the Bronx Zoo

Unlike thousands of horses "thundering
   across the prairie" to make us feel free,[†]
The handful of lemurs at the zoo,
Newly installed in small arboreal habitat
Meant to mimic their Madagascar home,
Seem like the spirits of primitive human
Beings, eerily complacent in captivity.

Unlike the thoroughly equine horse,
The mystical lemur has hands and feet
And mournful eyes that make us feel
Like cousins — if we discount
That prehensile tail, so deft as balance,
Hook, and rudder. Wouldn't people be better
Off with one of those?

O horse, with mane flung back
As you race the wind across the prairie,
Do not let yourself be locked
In paddock or pasture. O lemur,
Enclosed in cage, do not let the gawkers
Distract you as you receive signals
From a place beyond our ken.

---

† Dayton O. Hyde, Founder of Black Hills Wild Horse Sanctuary,
South Dakota, describing bands of mustangs crossing the prairie
haven.

Rabbit Ways

A cottontail resided in my yard,
a nimble forager,
nibbler of lettuce and dandelion.

My neighbor sicced his hound, Lutz, on him,
cursing his garden
incursions, begrudging his needs.

I offered sanctuary, studied his ways:
how he'd raise his head
from leafy repast, sniff the air,

rotate his ears like radar antennae, straining
for a sign of death —
bipedal, quadrupedal, or winged.

Hearing no danger, he'd resume feeding,
then in slo-mo
he'd hop a few feet for fresh forage.

Once at dusk we surprised each other
in the yard and froze,
eyeing each other. Minutes ticked by,

and then I dropped to all fours and pressed
my incisors to wild carrot.
He fed too, and then I slowly hopped

his way a foot or two and stopped,
raising my head to sniff
the air and rotate my rabbit ears,

and I heard the rush of fur and turned
to see Lutz leap
the bushy boundary between yards

and land on my frozen friend,
breaking his neck,
and then trot off with his trophy for his master.

Now the shortening summer days seem longer,
the dew damper,
as I forage on all fours, alone.

Fireflies

Where I grew up
we called them lightning bugs
and we loved them

like 4th of July fireworks —
only better, because they were
free and mysterious, benign

bugs that would land
on your shirt and plead
innocent, then fly

at the dark and blink
phosphorescent for a mate.
How few the nights

of their incandescence,
how few our own days
to blink.

Summer Carpenters

Those buzzing bees boring holes in the arbor
Aren't bumble bees, though they look alike
And sound alike. A bumble's body is fuzzy

While a borer's is slick black and the male lacks
A stinger; the female's less likely to use hers
Than a bumble female. The bumble will let you

Kneel inches away as you both work the garden,
But the borer will dive bomb anyone
Who enters its territory, even bounce

Off your head, buzzing all the while like an angry
Letter carrier with a heavy package to deliver.
Once inside an arbor beam, the borer hollows out

A chamber for eggs to hatch into larvae.
Hungry woodpeckers will excavate for a meal,
Their powerful beaks beating a tattoo

On your arbor and splintering its beams.
A dive-bombing borer bee or a drilling wood-
Pecker will test your love of nature

Like a bad case of poison ivy. Smoke
Out the borers at dusk and seal their holes.
Mark these words: No borers, no pecker birds.

Phragmites's Foe

Even the labors of Hercules
Included no task so epic
As defeating mighty Phragmites
On the banks of Long Pond.

Hacking and sawing away, you spent
The season bent over in knee-deep muck,
Obscure within the Greenbelt's woods
While others swam and sunned at the beach.

Why did you assume this thankless task,
Playing Mrs. Sisyphus,
The odds of extirpating this thick reed
No better than rolling that big stone

Up to the top of the hill without
The sickening thrill of seeing it
Tumble back down again and again,
Just as Phragmites will send shoots

Up from its watery base each spring?
Still, your work gave other, native, plants
A chance to reassert themselves
In the space you cleared on the bank.

For this your satisfaction came
From keeping your covenant
With Nature, to help keep invasives out
And let natives keep their tenuous grasp.

Glacial Warning

*"Norway's Breidablikkbrea glacier thinned by almost 3.1
metres during 2006 compared with 0.3 metres in 2005."*
— *Reuters, 16 March 2008*

How much longer till men and women,
Like miners hearing the song end
And seeing the canary's corpse,
Rush from the Earth cave to?

Miners scramble out of the mine
Gasping for fresh air, while we
Flounder from the encroaching ocean.
Some make it to high ground

But what habitation or work will they find?
Only a few scientists note Breidablikkbrea
Melting at ten times the rate from one year
To the next in once frigid Norway.

Walruses crowd shoulder to shoulder
On the shrinking ice floes, their tusks
Bright in the arctic sun in contrast
To their brown shaggy bodies.

Like the polar bears, these sea-loving
Mammals, once the melted floes
Can't support them, are, like a swimmer
Too far from shore, doomed to drown.

The adaptable Homo sapiens will
Migrate to higher ground where he can,
Leaving Long Islanders, Bangladeshi,
And the Dutch to the rising seas.

Summer Turns

After weeks of swelter
heat breaks
humidity dips

the breeze stiffens
with sea scent
Roadsides brim

with Queen Anne's lace
and goldenrod
Monarchs arrive

Apples turn
from toys
into serious fruit

The sun's slant
heightens color
deepens shade

and I feel the pang
the turn
toward fall can bring

Fall

Aftermath

It's not the storm itself — wind and rain lashing shore,
uprooting trees, toppling poles and dousing lights,
flooding cellars and roads, capsizing boats —
but the aftermath — the bright calm, the pair
of drowned cats crumpled against the picket fence,
the parlor of Izzy's shack open for inspection,
the walls fallen flat on all sides, your own
roof filling the front yard, covering your car,
and your own twin daughters dazed by Nature's
petulance — that makes you reconsider
your life and weigh your possessions and the cost
of putting down stakes too near the coast
as the globe warms, and storms grow worse.

Fall Upstate

Fall Upstate comes sooner, more sharply
Than on Long Island, two-hundred-miles south
And moderated by the Atlantic.

Fall Upstate turns cool the day after eighty
Degrees and September cumulus clouds
Make summer seem ceaseless. The south wind
Dies, chill Canadian air blasts in, and it's

Fall Upstate, and you pull on your down vest.
The green leaves turn scarlet before your eyes,
Insects drop dry husks on the window sill,

Casements open only mid-afternoons,
And Pendletons blanket beds ... but you know all
This, so I'm just blowing (wood) smoke to help
Us greet the insidious Downstate fall.

Night Light

Sharp cuts the knife of light at night
A thousand yards below our house
Where moonless nights have long been pitch
At least since Mohawk fires flared.

"We love the silent black nights,"
I'd tell our city friends in praise
Of this rural upstate haven. Now,
Because of some newcomer's fear of dark

A bright light illuminates his yard
And shines across a bale-strewn field
And into our bay window, dissolving
The illusion we are back to nature.

Despite this shrill artificial light
A semblance of silence still remains.

Autumn Scene

Downpour on Dog Hill Road
Sunday, October 1
Autumn leaves pastel in the rain

A wild turkey tom struts
Across the road
Soaked but aflame

Survival Mode

Pastel leaves fall through
The horse chestnut branches
Silent or rattling
Sliding or butterflying.

The trees hold their breath,
Undeluded that they'll soon be
Denuded, that without leaves
Causing the weight of snow

To break their boughs,
They'll best survive
The winter.

Barter

Fall at the summer house
on a hill two-hundred-miles
north of the city:

our field mowed, hay bales
stacked as in Brueghel,
fodder for the farmer's horses.

Drilling

Woodpecker drilling into wood
for food, drilling food
for thought into my head.

Raking Leaves

Bamboo teeth claw the fall leaves from my lawn,
Disinterring apple mummies, their skin
Gray with death; others squish like fresh dog shit
Under my heel, the aroma of rot
Blending with the leaves' fungal scent
On a raw day. I savor smells, season's
Bounty as much as the field's or orchard's,
And relish the tug of muscles grown slack
From too many days spent behind a desk.

Body at work, senses alert, I leave
The leaves in piles while imagination weaves
Images into phrases that give shape
To another harvest. Who knows which crop
Will mean the most when my rake at last drops?

Poets

Poets are gardeners —
Planters, pruners, gleaners —
Till they are mulch.

Fall's Sweep

Put summer in mothballs
Now fall's fresh air sweeps all —
Bluebirds, tomatoes, once-green
Leaves — into the big bin
Labeled "Winter."

Culling

Dozens of small apples rot in a mound
Amid their family trees, moth damaged
Fated never to mature.

I pick them off the grass or off the tree
After spotting frass of larvae, and toss
Host and pest onto the pile.

As I work, my spider's mind spins images
That I shall add to my pile of poems,
To ripen or to rot.

Such culling is the rule of life, of art;
To keep is easy, to discard is hard.

Acknowledgments

Many of the poems in this book were previously published in *Winged* (1995), *Grounded* (2005), *Phased* (2008), and *After Shakespeare: Selected Sonnets* (2011). Others appeared in the following publications, whose editors are gratefully acknowledged:

The Aurorean	"Drilling"
The Blackbird Review	"Birds of a Feather ..."
Blue Unicorn	"Crow(s)," "In the West Woods," "Marsh Marigold"
Free Verse	"Fall's Sweep," "Rabbit Ways"
Mid-America Poetry Review	"Autumn Scene," "Scavengers and Predators"
Möbius, The Poetry Magazine	"Glacial Warning"
Muddy River Review	"Barter," "Survival Mode"
The New Verse News	"Sad Birds"
Open Cut	"A Bird's Song"

Reeds and Rushes, ed. Kathleen Burgess. Columbus, Ohio: Pudding House Press, 2010.	"Phragmites's Foe"
Paumanok: Poems and Photographs of Long Island, ed. Kathaleen Donnelly. St. James, NY: Island Sound Press, 2009.	"Montauk Chiaroscuro"
Salt Marshes: A Natural and Unnatural History, Judith Weis, Carol A. Butler. New Brunswick, NJ: Rutgers University Press, 2009.	"Aftermath"
Sag Harbor Is a Literary Celebration, eds. Maryann Calendrille, Kathryn Szoka. Sag Harbor, NY: Harbor Electronic Publishing, 2006.	"Osprey"
Tiger's Eye	"The Tiger"
Waterways	"The Hudson," "Lemurs at the Bronx Zoo," "March 20, 2009," "Summer Carpenters," "Turtle Stamp"
Wilderness House Literary Review	"To a Tick"

About the Author

A seven-time Pushcart Prize nominee and a three-year Fulbright lecturer in Czechoslovakia, George Held taught English at Queens College for 37 years. His poems, short stories, book reviews, and translations have appeared in such places as *Circumference*, *Commonweal*, *Confrontation*, and *Notre Dame Review*, and on Garrison Keillor's *A Writer's Almanac*, as well as in more than two dozen anthologies. Held's seventeen poetry collections include *Beyond Renewal*, *After Shakespeare: Selected Sonnets*, and *Neighbors*, Books 1 and 2, animal poems for children, illustrated by Joung Un Kim. George lives in Greenwich Village with his wife, Cheryl.

About the Cover

David Freed, cover artist, is emeritus professor of art at Virginia Commonwealth University. He has work in collections at the Museum of Modern Art, Library of Congress, Philadelphia Museum of Art, San Francisco Museum of Art, Art Institute of Chicago, The Victoria and Albert Museum, and many others.

A NOTE ON THE TYPE

This book is set in Constantia, a serif typeface first conceived by John Hudson of Tiro Typeworks for Microsoft Corporation in 2003. Constantia is featured in the Microsoft ClearType Font Collection, a set of six fonts developed by exploiting leading-edge technology and embodying best in design practice to provide readable, attractive typefaces for either traditional print or on-screen use. Constantia utilizes the classical proportions of relatively small x-height and long extenders, as well as triangular-shaped or "wedge" serifs, making it an ideal choice for book and journal publishing. Its slight squareness and open counters ensure legibility even at smaller sizes. Sub-pixel positioning provides clearer on-screen rendering by using dithering at the RGB pixel level. ClearType, first introduced with Windows Vista and Office 2007, continues to be distributed with all newer versions of Office, various free Office viewers, the Microsoft Office Compatibility Pack and the Open XML File Format Converter for Mac.